Discover the Authentic Leader You Are Meant to Be

Alexa Starks

Contents

Dedication

I dedicate this book to my amazing husband, Wayne. Thank you for always believing in me and being my biggest cheerleader and my best friend. I love you endlessly.

Acknowledgments

I want to thank my husband for helping me with this book and getting my ideas out of my head, and my parents and my family for always cheering me on. I also want to thank Claremont Lincoln University for their incredible Master's degree program that inspired me to write this book based on my Capstone project. The program, professors, and curriculum were truly inspiring.

And always, in memory of Jake.

Introduction

You might be wondering, how is this leadership book different than all other leadership books? And honestly, that was the main question I asked myself when I wrote this book. How can I make this book different than all others because, shit, there are a LOT of books out there! This book is NOT the same as other leadership books because it requires your active participation in building leadership qualities and for personal development. This book requires you to participate in becoming the best version of yourself and growing your skills through self-reflection writing exercises. Yes—you will actually write in this book. For true personal development to grow into an authentic leader, you need to be engaged in your own growth, and that's exactly where this book can come in handy.

All other leadership books, leadership development programs, and self-help books try to fundamentally change who you are and what your core values are. They try to shape and mold you into something and someone else. They try to change you into someone who has x,y,z values that they think are important for leaders to have and want you to have x,y,z skills that good leaders should have. And that's all fine and dandy and valid that there are a set of skills, traits, characteristics and values that good leaders should have, but I truly believe that you can get nowhere in your journey to become a good leader without being your authentic self. After all, how can one be a leader if they have to copy what someone else does? It means leading is authentically based on YOUR core values, your morals and what you are passionate about.

Therefore, this book is about igniting your authentic leadership skills by increasing your self-awareness through several writing exercises (and, of course, with the help of the content in this book too). This book can help you tap into your self-awareness and discover your core values and how your experiences have shaped who you are today and what is important to you. Everyone is unique and special and has their own individual core values and morals, and that is what defines authentic leadership.

This book has a lot of valuable information to help you develop your authentic leadership skills and become the best version of yourself. It has a mix of information, personal stories (because I believe in being vulnerable and sharing my own personal stories to help you dive deep into your own experiences that have shaped who you are), and several writing exercises to help you develop your authentic leadership skills. I highly recommend that you take the time to complete the exercises I have included in the book so that they can help you achieve your authentic leadership goal.

And one last thing to clarify is who this book is for. This book is for anyone who wants to learn how to be a great leader, how to be grounded in their own core values and authentic leadership, and stay true to who they are. This is an actively engaging leadership journey that you will go on to uncover your leadership potential and more about who you are and how you can be the best version of yourself. This book is NOT for someone who already thinks they are the best they will ever be or consider themselves to be the greatest leaders. My goal is to teach you to be the best version of yourself in order to become the best leader that you can be and to grow personally and professionally!

You probably have noticed that most organizations preach their core values and important traits that a person should have. And that's great, but shouldn't you know what your core values are and your important traits before a company tries to push their ideal criteria on you? Absolutely yes. The bottom line is this book will help you to be a leader while staying true to who you are. It's an active participation leadership journey where you get to realize the leader that you can be and how you can be the best version of yourself. It will take some hard work, deep self-reflection, and writing.

And with that, I invite you to take on this journey of self-discovery of your own authentic leadership skills so that you can be a leader in everything that you do, even if you are not actually leading a team yet. Be a leader based on your own values, morals, and characteristics, and learn to lead authentically. Let's get started!

Chapter 1

What is Authentic Leadership?

Before we jump into what authentic leadership is, let's just do a quick refresh on the Introduction since I bet some of you skipped over that (and no need to feel guilty, I've done that many times as well). This book is for people looking to figure out their own style of leadership while staying grounded in their own core values, strengths and in doing what they love. This book requires your active participation in your own leadership journey. This means that it's not just generic advice for the masses; rather, it's uniquely tailored to help you discover your own values, strengths and skills and learn how to accomplish your goals while staying true to yourself. I start off by focusing on what makes you, you, with a lot of self-reflection writing exercises. It's going to take some work; you can't just read the pages and hope that it solves all of your problems without getting involved at all in any of the work. So, grab a pencil (Yes, you need to actually write in this book) and let's start working on you!

There are so many different leadership styles today, and a lot of them overlap in many traits. But I believe the best style is authentic leadership. It recognizes each individual as a unique person and helps you understand how you can lead authentically and be genuine and true to yourself.

In order to learn how to become an authentic leader, we first have to find out what authentic leadership is. Authentic leadership can be divided into significant aspects, which are:

1. Self-awareness of your core values, strengths, weaknesses, desires, thoughts, behaviors, and how your experiences have shaped who you are.
2. Always, ALWAYS acting transparently and in alignment with your core values in everything that you do personally and professionally[1].

The problem is if you don't have self-awareness of these aspects of yourself, then you often end up trying to copy people around you or emulate leaders who you admire. Or worse—you end up feeling uncertain of who you are, what you're meant to do and what you're passionate about. And as far as that is concerned, I've been there. It's often easier to look externally at others for inspiration or what career path you should take than it is to look internally at who you are and what you want. So first and foremost, you should know who you are and how you came to be the person that you are today. And in this regard, self-awareness can be of great help.

It's important to know what your strengths are because you can use them to your advantage or leverage them in situations to get ahead or do something better. Imagine if you didn't know how good you were at conflict resolution because you never tried or never had an opportunity to resolve a conflict between coworkers.

One day that situation might present itself, and you can step in and help them resolve something, or you can sit back and watch from afar because you don't know if you can help. Often we generally know what we're good at and what our strengths are. But sometimes we are so out of touch with our strengths, haven't honed our skills enough, or we're just not aware of them, and we don't use them every day. Now imagine the amazing things you could have done or accomplished had you realized your true potential and put all of your strengths to use!

Similarly, it's important to know what your weaknesses are so that you can work to improve them. It's not enjoyable when we're not good at something, and we dread being in a situation where we have to do that thing. Thus, personal development is all about finding ways that we can improve ourselves and how we can grow. If you could improve those areas of yourself so you could become an even better version of yourself, wouldn't you do that? I sure would! That's why it's important to have self-awareness of your weaknesses: so you can improve them. And that's exactly what we will work on in this book.

It's important to know what your core values are because they are fundamentally who you are and what you stand for. They guide your actions, whether you are aware of it or not, and they are shaped by your experiences in life. Your core values make up part of your character and what makes you, you. Being aware of how different experiences in your life have shaped you is important so that you can grow from those experiences and be aware of how they may change you, for better or worse. Good or bad life experiences impact us and can change who we are, but we can control what impact they can have on us in the long run.

Leading in alignment with your core values may sound easy, but it's about reliability and consistency. If your core value is integrity, that means others can rely on you for your honesty and consider you to be a person of integrity in every situation. As a leader, it's important for your team or company to see you project your core values in everything that you do. People need to see that you are who you say you are all of the time. That's consistency, and that's an incredibly important trait of authentic leadership.

So, let's focus on building self-awareness of your core values, strengths, weaknesses and then acting transparently and in alignment with those.

Let me quickly first share a personal story of my authentic leadership journey and how I developed my authentic leadership skills. It doesn't happen overnight, and no one taught me what my core values, strengths, or weaknesses were. I had to figure them out for myself. I've had a wonderful and tough life. My parents got divorced when I was a kid. I had bad depression in high school, and my younger brother committed suicide when I was in college. After he died, I spent several years bottling up all my emotions and feelings, and I was operating on autopilot every day, completely numb to everything. I literally felt like a mindless robot just going through the routine actions day after day.

Finally, I decided I didn't want to live like that anymore, and I started going to therapy. That's where I learned about self-awareness, meditation, and mindfulness exercises, and how to properly feel, express, and deal with all of my emotions. I'm happy to report that I no longer ever bottle up my emotions!

Anyways, it took a long time to discover what my core values, strengths, and weaknesses were. And I learned about all those through life experiences and self-reflection. My top three core values are honesty, kindness, and love.

However, I already knew what my core values were. I just didn't take the time to reflect on my past experiences and use my self-awareness to use my values to my advantage. My core value of honesty comes from my experiences of being lied to, feeling betrayed and never wanting to inflict that same harm and pain on anyone else. It also comes from knowing that being honest is not only ethically the right thing to do but that it benefits everyone, to be honest. Be honest about your feelings, thoughts, and actions. Your word has a lot of power behind it, and what you say or not say can have real implications. If you lie, it only comes back to hurt you in the end too, and while being honest can sometimes be hurtful, your word will hold more weight and will reflect a thousand times better on your character and integrity as a human. Your character and your words are a reflection of you and your core values. If you choose to lie or pick which situations to be honest in, then your character is flimsy.

My core values of kindness and love come from many years of doing community service and helping others. Feeling loved while seeing others not have that and wanting them to experience that kindness and love is where I derive my core values from. When you see someone in need of help, do you stop and help? I'm not talking about giving a dollar to someone with a cardboard sign on the side of the road. I mean, do you show kindness, compassion and empathy to everyone in all situations? Your core values need to be reflected in all of your actions, not just being compassionate to some people and not others. You can't cherry-pick when you use your core values because that's exactly why they are called "core values" - they are who you are to your core.

Alright, now that we know about core values, let's jump right into understanding how to develop yourself into an authentic leader. How do we discover your authentic leadership style? Well, this book uses reflection as a tool for building self-awareness of your core values, strengths, and weaknesses. There are several short writing exercises for you to complete, and these are incredibly important. Think of it as a short journaling exercise that will help you discover your own authentic leadership style that you can take with you to any job and everywhere else so you can apply it to your entire life.

You do not need to be in a leadership or managerial position to learn these skills and develop this awareness of who you are. You can be an authentic leader in everything that you do. Plus, you never know who is looking up to you…

Chapter 2
Self-Awareness

What is self-awareness? For the purpose of this book, we'll define self-awareness as actively and presently being aware of your thoughts, feelings, emotions, strengths, and weaknesses by using introspection or self-reflection. Simply put, it is being aware of yourself in the present moment[1]. Being self-aware means understanding what's going on in your mind and your body, where you feel it, and how strong the emotions and thoughts are. People with self-awareness use introspection and reflection to think about what their strengths and weaknesses are and then draw on their past experiences to determine their future approach.

Self-awareness means you need to think about what you're thinking about. You need to focus your mind, calm yourself down, be present and reflect on what's going on in your mind. A lot of people use meditation for the same purposes, which allows them to focus their attention and breath to turn off any distractions and focus on what is going on in their head.

I'll be the first to admit that I was very skeptical of meditation. I've always been a very active person, someone who is very loud, talkative, and has high energy. So the idea of sitting in silence for any length of time without moving was absolutely absurd and funny. Literally—I laughed so hard!

But then I realized that I didn't like being numb and on autopilot every day, unable to really feel deep happiness, love, or sadness. And so, I discovered meditation and mindfulness, which develop your self-awareness. Meditation helps you focus on the present moment and be aware of your body and surroundings, inherently drawing attention to what is going on in your body in the present moment. You can observe your thoughts and emotions because you're focused on the present moment, eventually enabling you to let it all go and focus on being present. Deep breathing exercises are part of meditation. Focusing your breath to center you in the present moment helps clear you of other thoughts as you focus your mind on your breath and not on the future or on overanalyzing the past.

To be honest, I was really bad at meditating at first. And it took A LOT of convincing for me even to try it for one minute. For the first few times, I could barely meditate for two minutes. Imagine sitting in silence and trying to clear your mind of any thoughts and it being so difficult that you want to give up. BUT DON'T GIVE UP! I highly recommend you try meditating, even if you just start with one minute of trying to clear your mind. Close your eyes, breathe slowly and calmly, and try to keep your mind clear. In order to keep yourself accountable for this practice, I recommend writing in a daily journal or planner. Start with 1 minute of meditation and write down that you meditated that day. Do that for a few days until you are able to meditate and clear your mind. Then slowly increase it to 2 minutes, and then 3 minutes, and so forth. If journaling isn't your thing, maybe set the alarm on your phone or a reminder to meditate every day at the same time each day, so it becomes part of your routine and daily habits.

Let's move on, though, and start working on you! Let's do some exercises aimed at increasing your self-awareness. We're going to start off by focusing on what makes you, you. This book is heavy on self-reflection and understanding yourself in order to understand what you actually need. It's going to take some work, but the important thing is that you actually participate and complete these writing exercises so you can be the leader of your own personal development. Consider these next few exercises your warm-up for the real work in the rest of the book. So, grab a pen or pencil, and let's start working on you!

So, let's begin with who are you? Take a moment, and on the next few pages, write down some things that come to your mind. Tell me about yourself! Describe yourself to someone who doesn't know you--like me! Tell me things that you like and don't like, what you like to do for fun, hobbies, passions, etc. Really take the time to reflect on who you are and how you are presenting yourself to the world.

This honestly took me some time as it might be the kind of assignment that is easier said than done. Let me give you some examples of my own:

1. I am a...foodie! I love to eat delicious food; pasta and dessert are my favorite foods, and I literally can never get bored of them. I like any kind of pasta and most kinds of desserts, like chocolate cake, ice cream, pastries, and cupcakes. If it's pasta/bread or carbs or sugary dessert, it's got my name on it!

2. I am...a gym rat! I used to call myself a runner since I trained to run half-marathons, full-marathons, and triathlons, but after a bit of knee pain and shin splints, I switched to lifting weights in the gym. It's a huge de-stressor for me that keeps my anxiety and stress low and helps me to be able to eat all the pasta and dessert that I want without worrying too much about gaining weight!

3. I am...funny! I laugh at my own jokes all the time. In fact, my husband laughs at me laughing at my own jokes, but secretly I think he finds me hilarious as well! I love to laugh; I love to get the giggles like a little kid or watch a comedy show and laugh my ass off. I believe laughing is incredibly healthy for you and brings a lot of positivity and light into your life. In some of my darkest and saddest moments in

life, I binge-watched comedy shows, like The Office, Parks and Recreation, and pretty much every stand-up comedy show on Netflix, to raise my spirits and bring me back up.

4. I am...super affectionate. I love to cuddle and snuggle up with my husband on the couch while we watch TV or cuddle in bed and be spooned all night. I love kisses and hugs and being wrapped up in the giant biceps and pecs of my husband! (Sorry, TMI, I couldn't help it!) But honestly, I've been in relationships where the other person was not as affectionate as I was, and I always felt that they didn't love me back or that there was something wrong with me. **You have to know yourself and what you need,** and in my case, I know I need affection. I give affection, and my husband gives me back just as much affection, and it's an amazing feeling to have that.

Alright, enough about me now. Take some time on the next few pages and tell me about yourself. Take this time to really do some deep self-reflection on who you are, what you love, what your interests are, etc. Allow this exercise to really get to know yourself so that you can better understand what you need in order to be successful/happy in life.

I am...

My hobbies/interests are… OR I love to…

Now try to wrap it all up in one or two sentences to describe yourself! For example, I am an affectionate, hilarious foodie and gym rat! Or I am a foodie and gym rat, and I am hilarious and affectionate!

____

____

____

____

____

____

Now comes the harder part! Was that exercise difficult for you? Which part was difficult, or was it all difficult? It didn't have to be all positive and frou-frou if that's not how you're feeling about yourself at this moment. I want you to be authentic and honest with yourself, as that's the only way to grow. I'm not judging you; no one is judging you here; this is a safe space. (And if anyone ever judges you for anything, you can politely tell them to go fuck off!). It's absolutely okay if some of your descriptions of yourself aren't as positive because that just means that you have plenty of room to grow, and you can only go up from here. Perhaps you wrote, "I am... frustrated / sad / depressed / angry / stuck / whatever" or "My hobbies are... sleeping all day / doing nothing / being anti-social." The goal of this exercise is to start building your self-awareness and reflect on who you are, what you love to do or don't love to do, what your hobbies, interests, or passions are, etc. I want you to start building self-awareness (literal awareness of yourself!) and explore your key strengths, dreams, and goals. So, if you skipped any of those exercises on the previous pages, please go back and complete them. All of the exercises in this book are to *help you!* **It doesn't work as well if you half-ass your own help.**

Now that you've completed the exercises and have a better understanding of who you are let's talk about your problems. What is bothering you that you want to fix? Or what isn't going so well in your life that you'd like to improve? Or what are the goals that you want to accomplish but can't seem to figure out how?

Another purpose of this exercise is to build your self-awareness so that you can reflect on what you are missing or needing that convinced you to read a self-help/leadership book. Think deeply about what exactly your "problem" or "obstacle" is, try to put it into words, and be as descriptive as possible. After that, I want you to write down what the ideal outcome or solution would be in your opinion, and again, please be as descriptive and specific as possible here.

For example, years ago when I used to read a lot of self-help books, I would have written, "My problem is I am unhappy, unmotivated, and I feel like I am missing something in my life because it feels empty and sad." Then, I would have put my solution as "I want to find happiness and love and have a fulfilling and meaningful life." In this example, I am describing a problem and a solution, but the solution is still a little bit vague and not as **quantifiable,** i.e., can I measure this successfully. Now, notice how I could try to make it a little more specific and quantifiable. For example, "I want to be happy, love myself, have a happy and loving relationship, and find a job that is fulfilling and satisfying so I don't hate going to work every day." That's definitely more quantifiable and measurable; although still not 100%, it's better than the first solution!

I can work towards having more self-love and finding a happy, loving relationship, and I can interview for jobs that I find more fulfilling and meaningful than my current job.

So, I want you to write down your problems or challenges and then the solution. Please be as specific and descriptive as possible. And make sure to offer quantifiable (measurable) solutions. Take your time on this and really reflect on what you want or what isn't going right for you and what can be a solution for these problems.

My Problem/Obstacle/Need is…

____

____

____

____

____

____

My solution/outcome/desire is…

____

____

____

____

____

Before jumping to actionable steps that you should take to achieve these goals or overcome these problems, let's work our way through the rest of the book and then come back to this. The rest of the book focuses on continuing to develop your self-awareness, important aspects of your character, your core values, and strengths, and boost your personal growth and development. Keep an open mind and heart, and remember that this book isn't just generic advice. Rather, it's uniquely tailored to help you learn how to solve your own problems and achieve your own unique goals and progress in life. This book will help you unlock and discover how you can be the best version of yourself, the best leader that you can be, and how you can accomplish all of your goals.

For now, let's continue with a few more self-awareness exercises and discover who you are! Reminder: consider these as a warm-up to the rest of the book, so please make sure to do them!

Take a deep breath and focus on the thoughts that are running through your mind. Write down all of the thoughts going on in your mind in this present moment. No judgment of the thoughts; just simply write down the things that you are thinking about right now:

1. ______________________________

2. ______________________________

3. ______________________________

4. ______________________________

5. ______________________________

6. ______________________________

7. ______________________________

8. ______________________________

9. ______________________________

10. ______________________________

Now do the same exercise but with your emotions. Write down what emotions you are feeling right now. Write down the feelings that are associated with any thoughts. For example, are you feeling anxious, excited, nervous, fearful, courageous, hurt, happy, in love, sad, etc.? Focus entirely on any emotions and feelings that you are experiencing in this present moment related to the thoughts you listed above. Even if these emotions do not relate to the above thoughts at all and they are just random emotions, note them down.

1. ____

2. ____

3. ____

4. ____

5. ____

6. ____

7. ____

8. ____

9. ____

10. ____

Now take that list of emotions above and pick only a few of them, maybe the really strong emotions, and write down where you feel the emotion manifest in your body. For example, when I am anxious, I feel it in my chest and the pit of my stomach. Or, when I'm really happy, I feel it in my cheeks and my eyes because I smile really big. So, pick a few (or all) of the emotions that you listed above (the ones you are feeling in this present moment), and write down where you are feeling these emotions in your body.

1. Emotion:

____

Where are you feeling it?

____

2. Emotion:

____

Where are you feeling it?

____

3. Emotion

____

Where are you feeling it?

____

4. Emotion:

____

Where are you feeling it?

____

Write down any activities or actions that make you really happy. Think of the moments when you have been really happy and think about what you were doing in those moments. For example, maybe running makes you happy, or cooking, or singing in the shower. Maybe it's spending time with your significant other, or maybe it's reading an excellent book. List down the moments when you were happy and what made you happy.

1. ______________________________________

2. ______________________________________

3. ______________________________________

4. ______________________________________

5. ______________________________________

6. ______________________________________

7. ______________________________________

8. ______________________________________

9. ______________________________________

10. _____________________________________

Alrighty, I am super proud of the work you just put in those last few pages. That was a lot of self-reflection work, and you are beginning to flex your self-awareness muscles. Do you want to know a secret? I was going to therapy and was talking about my anxiety, and my therapist actually helped me with this exercise. She had me explain where I felt the anxiety in my body, and I told her that I felt it in my chest and my chest would get tight. I was then more aware of my chest being tight when I was anxious again. But the crazy part was she explained to me that my chest was feeling tight because I wasn't breathing properly when I was anxious. I'd hold my breath for long periods of time, and I didn't even know I was doing that! The next time I felt anxious, I made a conscious effort to focus on my breathing, and I breathed in for three counts and out for three counts, and my anxiety actually decreased! So...the moral of the story is this: self-awareness is really important! Keep reading and keep doing the exercises in this book!

Another exercise! What makes you sad or angry, and how do you cope with it? What do you do to cheer yourself back up again, or how do you deal with that emotion? It's okay to feel sad and upset; those are natural responses to things in our lives, and you shouldn't bottle them up. Let yourself feel those emotions, process them, feel where they are in your body, and then work through them so you can come out stronger on the other side.

For example, what makes me sad is missing my brother, who committed suicide a few years ago. The sadness comes and goes, but when I feel sad, I let myself feel sad for a few minutes, maybe cry it out if I need to, and then I try to think of a happy memory of him.

Another example is sometimes when I'm just feeling super moody, grumpy, mad, and sad for no reason at all (probably hormones!) I watch a funny TV show or a stand-up comedy show to cheer myself up until I feel better.

So…what makes you sad or angry or upset, and how do you cope with it and cheer yourself up? It's important for building your self-awareness to understand all of your emotions and how you cope or work through them.

____

____

____

____

____

____

Phew! Great work on these self-awareness exercises. If you're asking yourself what this has to do with leadership development, think of these exercises as your warm-up to the rest of the book. The rest of the book continues with these self-awareness and self-reflection exercises where you need to dive deep into who you are and various aspects of yourself, and it's important to be open and honest with yourself about who you are. It's important to know what makes you, you! It's important to know what makes you happy or sad or how you deal with intense emotions because emotional intelligence is very important for being a good leader. So, now that we're all warmed up let's jump into the meat and potatoes of your authentic leadership journey and become the best version of yourself and all that you can be!

Chapter 3
Core Values

Now that we've started to work on developing your self-awareness by doing some simple and easy self-reflection writing exercises, let's jump right into the meat of authentic leadership: your positive core values.

Your core values define who you are at your deepest level. They define your character and what you stand for. They are the deeply held beliefs that are of utmost importance to you and often dictate how you behave and act, consciously or subconsciously. Sometimes, core values are something that you learned in your childhood, for instance, being nice to others or not lying (even about brushing your teeth or that you ate all your vegetables instead of giving them to the dog).

For example, my top core values are honesty, kindness, love, and fairness. This practically means that I am always honest and truthful, and I present myself genuinely instead of pretending or lying. I'm very kind and compassionate and always show others kindness, and I love and care about others and have empathy for others. I also always try to be fair and give everyone a fair chance and equal opportunities. These core values guide my decisions and actions in both personal and professional settings. Furthermore, these are not core values that I can pick and choose when I want to use them. I cannot be just kind and honest in one situation and then lie and be cruel in another situation. So these core values guide my behavior and my thinking, and how I perceive the world and act accordingly.

Now the question is why it's important to know your core values. You most likely know your core values subconsciously or aren't really aware of them at all, but they have likely been a part of you. They have shaped your experiences so far in your life, and your experiences have shaped your core values and who you are in turn. But it's important to understand how your life and experiences have shaped who you are. For example, maybe you had a situation where someone asked you to lie, but it just felt so wrong, and you were so distressed by lying that you told the truth. You decided to be honest because it felt like the right thing to do. Honesty and integrity might then be two of the core values that you live by, and you use them as your guiding principles in your actions and decisions. Likewise, perhaps you are a compassionate person who loves helping others in need, and you've spent a lot of time doing community service because you wanted to. In this case, compassion is likely to be one of your core values.

Knowing what your core values are and using your self-awareness to reflect on past experiences in your life is important to guide your actions into the future. Reflecting on past experiences will also help clarify what your core values are and how they came to be. Thus, no more living on autopilot and being unaware of your actions and intentions. It's time to know who you are and what you stand for.

So, let's work on defining and clarifying your core values. Maybe you already have an idea of what they are, or maybe you don't. Here is a list of some top personal positive core values:

Adaptability	Innovation	Sensitivity
Honesty	Relationships	Fairness
Optimism	Creativity	Leadership
Ambition	Inspiring/	Strength
Hope	Motivating	Flexibility
Originality	Resilience	Learning
Bold/Fierce	Determination/	Supportive
Humility	Discipline	Generosity
Passion	Integrity	Love
Challenges	Empathy	Trust
Humor	Intelligence	Gratitude
Patience	Vision	Loyalty
Compassion	Energy	Uniqueness
Individuality	Intuition	Happiness
Personal Growth	Risk-taking	Openness
Courage	Ethical	Resourcefulness
	Kindness	

Read through the above list and write down your top 10 core values. Just write down 10 that stick out to you when you think about the values that define who you are.

1. _______________________________

2. _______________________________

3. _______________________________

4. _______________________________

5. _______________________________

6. _______________________________

7. _______________________________

8. _______________________________

9. _______________________________

10. ______________________________

Now consider the list of your top 10 core values and pick 5 values among these that are most important to you and that define who you are. These 5 values should be the ones that guide you in your life, define what you stand for, and what drives most of your actions and behaviors.

Note: This took me a long time to boil it down to just 5! Agh! That was like picking just my top 5 favorite foods out of my top 10 favorites; they're all my favorite! But seriously, this exercise helps you narrow down the *5 most important core values* to you, so take all the time that you need to choose.

1. ____

2. ____

3. ____

4. ____

5. ____

Now, from the above top 5 core values, pick your **top 3** that you could not live without. These 3 core values should truly and deeply shape who you are and your actions. Not only do these core values define your character but also everything you do.

1. ____

2. ____

3. ____

If you are stuck at all 5 core values and couldn't whittle it down to just 3, that is completely fine as well. I have more than 4 core values that shape and define who I am. That said, I do have my top and most important 3 values that I mentioned previously at the beginning of the book (honesty, kindness, love). For now, though, keep your top 5 or your top 3 if you were able to narrow it down to three.

The next few writing exercises are designed to help you clarify and solidify those core values that you chose. Be very thoughtful and reflective when you write. These are designed to help you recognize your core values in your actions.

Write down your top 10 important, impactful, or defining moments in your life. These can be good or bad experiences. Maybe they changed your life completely or just slightly reshaped your life and who you are. Maybe it was losing a loved one or someone close to you, winning an award or sports event, graduating college, etc. Think of 10 really important experiences and moments in your life. While you're writing down each experience, reflect on why it was an impactful experience. Just think about it.

For example, an impactful moment in my life was running a marathon. (In my mind, I'm reflecting that it was important because I didn't believe that I could run that much, but I trained hard for it, so when I crossed that finish line, it was incredibly rewarding and fulfilling to do what I didn't think I could do). A few other impactful moments in my life were when my parents divorced when I was 7 because it changed how I grew up, my brother dying when I was 21 fundamentally changed who I was and who I am today, graduating college, getting a graduate degree, meeting the love of my life (my amazing husband!), etc., etc. *Think about the impactful moments in your life that have changed who you are or have made you who you are today.*

1. ______________________________

2. ______________________________

3. ______________________________

4. ______________________________

5. ______________________________

6. ______________________________

7. ______________________________

8. ______________________________

9. ______________________________

10. ______________________________

Now, consider the above-mentioned top 10 important or impactful moments and experiences in your life and shortlist just the top 5 most important and most impactful. Maybe these are the ones that fundamentally changed or shaped who you are in your life. Maybe they helped you see something differently. Maybe they are good or bad, happy or sad moments, but choose just the 5 most important and impactful moments/experiences in your life from that list of 10.

1. ____

2. ____

3. ____

4. ____

5. ____

Now, for each of those 5 moments, write down the core values that you exhibited in those experiences. Either the core values that got you to that moment or you used in the moment or the core values that you learned from that experience. For example, if graduating college was one of your 5 impactful moments, and maybe you listed perseverance as one of your core values, write that down. Maybe it's hard work or dedication or discipline. If one of your impactful moments was losing a loved one, maybe one of the core values you learned from that experience is resilience, optimism, or compassion.

You can absolutely list more than one core value for each experience as well! You don't have to limit yourself. This exercise is just designed to help you solidify and clarify your core values and how you learned them from different life-shaping experiences or how you've already used them in the important moments in your life.

For example, my brother committing suicide is one of my top 5 impactful moments, and I'd write down a core value of compassion and kindness because that moment shaped me to be even more compassionate towards others and help others. I also learned that I had to use resilience to get through it, so I might write that down too. Another example of my top impactful moments was meeting my husband because it helped teach me what true love is and what love can be and should be when it's so healthy and wonderful. This impactful moment filled my life with even more love that I can share with him and with those around me. Soooo…your turn!

Important Moment #1:

____

Core Value:

____

Important Moment #2:

____

Core Value:

____

Important Moment #3:

____

Core Value:

____

Important Moment #4:

____

Core Value:

____

Important Moment #5:

____

Core Value:

____

Great job with all those writing exercises! If you did NOT do the writing exercises, please go back and do them. They are designed to truly help you understand who you are at your core and to help you recognize how your experiences have shaped who you are today.

Continue to do these exercises throughout your life as a "check-in" on yourself. Maybe you'll find that in 10 years, you're a different person based on new life experiences that have changed who you are. Or maybe you've lost who you are and need to reconnect with yourself. Either way, I hope you have a bit more awareness and knowledge now of who you are and what you can be in the future.

Chapter 4

Strengths and Weaknesses

You know intuitively what your strengths and weaknesses already are without having to read a book or take a quiz to inform you about what you already subconsciously or consciously know. For example, you know what your weaknesses are because it's usually the things you try to avoid or are fearful of doing, or every time you have to do them, it drains your energy. For example, maybe one of your weaknesses is that you're not a good public speaker, which means, whether you are aware of it or not, you usually try to avoid public speaking whenever possible. Or maybe one of your weaknesses is that you aren't very good at emotional regulation. You often have outbursts of anger or frustration, and if you paid attention, you'd see the negative reactions around you from your team members or friends.

So, we're going to do a similar exercise as all the other writing exercises in this book and do some self-reflection! Yay! Here are some top leadership strengths and weaknesses that leaders generally have:

Strengths	Weaknesses
Self-Awareness	Lack of Trust
Emotional Intelligence	Micromanaging
Integrity	Lack of Integrity
Good communication Skills	Being Closed-Minded or Inflexible
Conflict Resolution Skills	Insecurity
Public Speaking skills	Lack of Empathy
Flexibility	Being Unrealistic
Confidence	Hypocrisy – saying one thing but not doing it yourself
Hard work/ Perseverance/ Determination	Lack of Accountability

The list can go on and on… but it's crucially important (as we've discussed earlier) to be aware of our strengths and weaknesses. With this awareness, we can not only leverage our strengths to be great leaders and continue building upon those strengths to make them stronger but also work on fixing and correcting our weaknesses and shortcomings. Check out how one of the important leadership strengths is self-awareness, which is exactly what we've been working on so far in the book to help develop it in you! There are also strengths specific to your profession, like change management, networking, problem solving, creativity, project management, strategic thinking, coaching, and so much more. Also, some of your core values can also be strengths, so reflect back on what you wrote down earlier. Furthermore, some of your weaknesses might be the strengths listed in the above table if you aren't good at them, like public speaking, emotional intelligence, or communication skills.

I'm going to define a few of these for you because they are really important to be aware of:

Emotional Intelligence – recognizing, understanding, and managing our own emotions and others' and the impact our behavior and emotions can have on other people[1].

Integrity – being honest, doing the right or ethical thing, and being grounded in strong moral principles (think again about your core values exercises!)

Good Communication Skills – clearly communicating your thoughts, ideas, or feelings in a healthy and constructive way, but also actively listening to the other person and letting them speak all their thoughts—and understanding—what they are saying.

Flexibility – being able to quickly pivot, change, or adapt to new or different situations. As a leader, you need to be flexible to different challenges, people, and situations. Don't get too bogged down and set in your ways.

Lack of Trust – this comes down to not trusting yourself or others to get the job done, tell the truth, or do what you need them to do. This is often evident in leaders who tend to micromanage people and need to look over their shoulders or have all work go through them for approval. You need to trust people and your employees and create a culture of trust and positive relationships.

Insecurity – this is similar to lack of trust, but being insecure means, you usually aren't very aware of it. So when it comes to trusting others, you find it difficult to trust them because you really don't trust yourself or know what you're talking about. This often leads you to lash out at others, or become insecure about your abilities, so you get angry or take it out on others.

Alrighty, so let's dive into our self-reflection exercises now like we have in the previous chapters and focus on you. Really take the time to be honest to yourself, be vulnerable with yourself, and look inside yourself. There's no downside at all to these exercises because when we identify those "weaknesses," only then can we start to learn how to change them and become a stronger, better person and grow our skills! There's only one way to go from here, and it's up! Again, please do these writing exercises, whether it's in pen or pencil, I do not care, but this is for your benefit so you can get unique insights into what is truly tailored for you and your abilities in life. Alright, let's jump in:

Think about some of the best or most rewarding moments in your career or in your life. These moments have to be ones when you either accomplished something huge or did something amazing at work. Think about the strengths that you used or exhibited in these moments. For example, in one of my jobs early in my career, I started going to Toastmasters to become a better public speaker, and I loved it. One day at work, they were doing a week-long leadership training program, and I asked my boss to have me signed up for it, and he did. I was able to use the public speaking skills that I had been working on to be much more vocal in the course and stand out as a leader in that program. And not just that, I also had such an amazing time and learned so much. I might also say that a big personal accomplishment was running a marathon, and I used perseverance and determination to achieve that.

So, what are some amazing or rewarding moments in your career or life, and what strength did you use to achieve them? (You don't have to just use the list of strengths above, be creative and reflect on YOUR strengths and what you do best! You may also use a core value if it fits here)

1. Moment:

Strength:

2. Moment:

 Strength:

3. Moment:

Strength:

4. Moment:

Strength:

5. Moment:

Strength:

Take a few moments here to really reflect on those exceptionally great moments in your career or life and be proud of yourself for what you've accomplished. Be proud of the strengths that you have and have shown in your work or with others!

So, if you had to write down your top 5 strengths, what would they be? (Again, these don't just have to be from the list of strengths above, look inside yourself at what your strengths are and what you do the best!)

1. _______________________________________

2. _______________________________________

3. _______________________________________

4. _______________________________________

5. _______________________________________

Now, let's do a similar exercise and consider these strengths and think about where you want to be in your career one day or the things you want to accomplish with the help of these strengths. Write down the strengths you would use to accomplish it or to get there and how you will use that strength. For example, if you want to be promoted to Director of Marketing, you might have to use your excellent communication skills and your creativity because you'll need to design marketing processes and documents and work with different teams to get insight or help from others etc., etc.

So, what are some things that you want to accomplish in the future, whether it's personal or professional, and what strengths will you use to achieve them?

1. Goal:

____

Strength:

____

2. Goal:

____

 Strength:

____

3. Goal:

____

Strength:

____

Great work! You don't need to write down all of your goals just yet; we'll get to that in the next chapter. I just want you to start thinking about how you can use your strengths to your advantage to achieve your goals. If you don't have self-awareness of what your strengths are, it makes it harder to achieve your goals. So awareness of your strengths and how you can use them is the first step and the ultimate key here.

Now, let's do some work on your weaknesses. We're going to work on improving your weaknesses, but again, the first step is awareness of what they are. So, think about the aspects of you that could use some improvement. How are your leadership skills or your relationships at work or in your personal life? Maybe you need more self-confidence or self-love that you can work on. What are you not good at? For example, maybe you aren't good at controlling your emotions, and in meetings, you often have an outburst of anger and get visibly frustrated and upset. That might be an area that could use some improvement so you can better control your emotions, especially the negative ones, and productively communicate your thoughts without getting overwhelmed and upset. I used to be bad at emotional intelligence because of all the pain in my life and bottling up my emotions. But after therapy, finding meditation, and working on expressing my emotions, I now have much better emotional intelligence skills, can clearly express my own emotions, and understand how to recognize others' emotions better. This helps me be a better leader to help my team deal with challenges or conflicts.

So, what are some of your weaknesses or areas that need some improvement in your life, personally or professionally? Take the time here to really reflect on what you would like to work on to improve yourself. Be honest with yourself about who you are and everything about yourself. There's nothing to be ashamed of or mad about here, just be yourself and use your self-awareness skills. Your weaknesses/areas of improvement are:

1. ____

2. ____

3. ____

4. ____

5. ____

Woohoo! If you wrote down 5 things that you want to improve, I'm incredibly proud of you. If you skipped this section… tsk tsk… go back and do them, please. It's only meant to help you become the best version of yourself, and that means improving areas of yourself that could use a little tune-up.

Let's take those 5 weaknesses that you wrote down above and now write what it would look like if those things improved. For example, if "good communication skills" were something that you need to improve, what would it look like if you did improve it? Does it mean you can clearly express your thoughts or feelings to others? Does it mean you can resolve conflicts easier and better because you can communicate more clearly? Or if you wrote down a weakness of "procrastinating" and you were to improve it, it might look like you are being able to get more work done in a day, be part of more projects at work, and potentially get the raise or promotion that you want.

So, take those weak areas needing improvement and write down what it would look like if these were no longer weaknesses and you did "fix" these or improved them:

1. Weakness:

____

What it looks like when improved:

____

2. Weakness:

____

 What it looks like when improved:

____

3. Weakness:

____

What it looks like when improved:

____

4. Weakness:

____

What it looks like when improved:

____

5. Weakness:

____

What it looks like when improved:

____

Great work, everyone! Again, please be sure you actually did these exercises so that you can be the best version of yourself and improve every aspect of who you are! In the next chapter, we are going to work on how we actually get to that improvement and the steps we need to take to achieve our goals and make personal developments.

Chapter 5

Designing Your Future

Before we dig in, let's talk about how we achieve goals. First, they need to be quantifiable in some way, so you know when you've actually "achieved" that goal! Regardless of if it's personal or professional goals, they need to be quantifiable and easy to recognize when you have achieved that goal. Second, you need to work backward. Figure out what you want, and then work backward on what you would actually need to do to get there. This will take work, time, patience, perseverance, discipline, and dedication. Personal or professional development doesn't happen overnight, but you must not give up too easily. Third, the goal must be realistic. Don't set a goal like "become an astronaut" when you've never taken a physics class in your life, and you get nauseous when you fly in a plane because it'll be nearly impossible for you to become an astronaut (not completely impossible, but highly unlikely). So set realistic goals that you can achieve with hard work, dedication, and patience. And lastly, once you reach your goal and achieve what you wanted, set your next goal. Never stop working on yourself and improving yourself and your skills or learning new things. Set goals that are challenging and maybe a little scary because you only grow when you're out of your comfort zone!

Alright, so let's get into designing your future and how you can become the best version of yourself! Let's take it back to the beginning of this book: what your problem/ obstacle/ challenge is and what your desired solution/outcome is. Clearly, you're not reading this book if you already think that you're the best leader that ever walked this planet. There must be something that compelled you to read this book, and there is something in your life that you want to improve upon or be better at. So, what was that solution/ outcome that you wrote about in Chapter 2? Let's try to sum it up in a sentence.

My solution/outcome to the problem is:

____

____

____

Great, now let's figure out how we work backward from there. What step must you take immediately before you accomplish that solution/ outcome to the problem? And then what is the step right before that step in order to accomplish that one? And so on and so forth… These should be exactly the steps you would need to get to the next step until you reach your desired outcome. One of the examples that I gave as my desired outcome/ solution to my previous reason of unhappiness/ lack of motivation years ago was, "I want to be happy and love myself and have a happy and loving relationship and find a job that is fulfilling and satisfying, so I don't hate going to work every day." Okay, so these are really two separate goals: having a happy and loving relationship and having a fulfilling, enjoyable job. Let's take both here **and work backward** (so you'd read this as 4,3,2,1):

1. I want to have a happy and loving relationship.
2. Find/be with someone that does meet my needs that I realized (my amazing husband!)
3. That means I might need to break up with my current significant other because they are not the right person for me, and be happy on my own until I find my person.
4. I need to figure out what "the right person for me" means: do I need someone who is a better lover or is more in touch with their emotions or affectionate, or someone who communicates better, or someone who doesn't party as much, etc. Figure out what I need in a relationship and from a partner (this means self-reflection!) **This is the first step in the process where you would start in order to achieve your goal. Remember, we work backward!**

1. Have a fulfilling and enjoyable job

2. Find a job that I find fulfilling and enjoyable, i.e., quit my current job and interview for new jobs or switch roles at my current company to something more fulfilling and enjoyable.

3. Figure out what I am passionate about or what career/ job I would find fulfilling and enjoyable (this means self-reflection!) **This is the first step in the process where you would start in order to achieve your goal. Again remember, we work backward!**

So take a moment to think about the steps you would need to take, work backward from your desired solution/ outcome to the problem that you wrote back in Chapter 2, and work backward to how you would accomplish that.

My solution/outcome to the problem is:

Working backward, I must:

1. ____

2. ____

3. ____

4. ____

5. ____

If that was tough or challenging, good! Growth happens when we challenge ourselves. Also, we can't really achieve our goals if we don't really figure out how we accomplish them and the steps we need to take. Otherwise, we end up just wandering aimlessly, lacking motivation, or feeling meh. Make sure you read those steps backward, so 5, 4, 3, 2, and 1 to make sure they all line up to that goal at #1.

Alright, next, let's do some core value work again, and we'll come back to the goal-setting. Think back to what your top 3 core values were (or you can flip back to the page where you wrote it down in the exercise!).

1. ____

2. ____

3. ____

Now, let's turn them towards the future. You previously wrote about past experiences or moments where you used those core values, but now let's write the future. Take each core value and write a scenario where you use that core value. Get into details about how you use that core value as a leader or to do good or help others. Try to write more than one sentence; write a few sentences about how you would use that core value in a specific moment.

For example, one of my core values is honesty. In a future scenario, perhaps I am a team leader, and it's time for annual performance reviews. As much as my other core value of kindness makes me want to just say only nice things, there may be a situation where I need to be honest. I'd be honest with this team member about their performance—but in a kind way, not mean or rude—

and will provide them with the resources they might need to improve their performance. If I'm not honest with them, then they cannot grow and improve themselves. In another example, one of my core values is kindness and compassion, and let's go with a personal example. Suppose someone who I do not like comes to me asking for my help or advice about something. Rather than turning them away (and saying, "fuck off," which is really tempting sometimes!) I will use my kindness to recognize that they came to me from a place where they need my help, so I will help them. That doesn't mean I have to like them, though! It just means that I am kind enough to help others.

So, take each of your three core values and write a scenario where you use your core value in a real-life example, personal or professional.

Core Value 1:

____

A real-life future scenario where you use that core value:

____

____

Core Value 2:

____

A real-life future scenario where you use that core value:

____

____

Core Value 3:

____

A real-life future scenario where you use that core value:

____

____

Fantastic work! That was also a tough exercise, and I'm proud of the work that you've done throughout this whole book. Being able to understand how past experiences have been impactful in shaping who you are today and what your core values are and then being able to apply those core values to future scenarios is incredible. This means you can act in alignment with your core values because you understand what your core values are, which is part of authentic leadership! Make sure to always keep practicing these exercises throughout your career and life; your core values may shift in importance as you go through life and experience new things, so check in with yourself often to see where you are, how you've grown, how your new experiences have impacted who you are and your core values.

Now we're going to do a similar exercise about your strengths from the previous chapter, but a slightly different writing exercise. Think again about your top 5 strengths and write them down:

1. ____

2. ____

3. ____

4. ____

5. ____

Great, now let's think about how you can use one or more of these strengths to become a better leader, whether it's now or in the future. How can you use one or more of your strengths to be a great leader, and what does that look like? How do you help others or your team? How do you be a leader and spread goodness, and be an inspiration that others can look up to as a great leader? How do you help others to also become the best versions of themselves when you are their leader? Take the time to really think about this one and how you will use your strengths to not only be the best version of yourself but also inspire others to do the same.

Fantastic work! That was a tough one! If you need to go back to it and re-write parts of it, that is totally acceptable! The above exercise focuses on applying what you've uncovered and learned about yourself and how you can be the best leader and the best version of yourself. A great leader inspires others to also be the best versions of themselves and to constantly learn and grow personally and professionally.

Next, let's do a bit more work on those weaknesses/ areas of improvement and how we can actually improve them! In one sentence, write down again what your 5 weaknesses/ areas of improvement are and what it looks like when improved. For example, "not micromanaging and trusting my team to do their job and being more hands-off."

1. ____

2. ____

3. ____

4. ____

5. ____

Now, let's do our exercise about working backward in order to accomplish the goal. What steps do you need to take in order to actually change these weaknesses/ areas of improvement? What do you need to do to improve your skills and grow? Is it taking a course on how to trust others better, or maybe going to therapy to work through trust issues from your past, or taking a leadership course about how to be a better manager? Is it having a conversation with your team about what you would need them to do so you can lead them better based on what they actually need?

Do your goal-setting work backward that we did earlier in this chapter: you already know what that weakness would look like if you improved it. Now figure out what steps you actually need to take to get there. Perhaps it's therapy. Perhaps it's taking a course or reading a book about it. Perhaps it's shadowing someone at your company to learn from them. Think about the exact steps and work backward:

1. Weakness:

____

What it looks like when improved:

____

Working backward, I must:

____

____

____

2. Weakness:

____

 What it looks like when improved:

____

 Working backward, I must:

____

____

____

3. Weakness:

____

What it looks like when improved:

____

Working backward, I must:

____

____

____

4. Weakness:

____

 What it looks like when improved:

____

Working backward, I must:

____

____

____

5. Weakness:

____

What it looks like when improved:

____

Working backward, I must:

____

____

Remember that you want to work backward and be as specific as possible with the real steps that you need to take so that when you finish reading this book, you know exactly what you need to do in order to improve upon those weaknesses/ areas of improvement and work to become the best version of yourself and a great leader! If that exercise was challenging, good! It's meant to be tough because working on yourself is always going to be a little uncomfortable, and we only grow when we push ourselves and get out of our comfort zone and challenge ourselves to learn and grow and become the best versions of ourselves that we can be.

Alrighty, everyone, this is the last exercise that you will do in this chapter. I am incredibly proud of the hard work that you've put in, the self-reflection, the self-awareness that you've developed of who you are, all that you can be, and the great leader you can discover inside of you! You can now be the authentic leader rooted in your core values, your strengths, shaped by your emotions and your experiences, and become the best possible YOU!

So, that said, let's wrap it all up in one final writing exercise that brings it all together.

Picture yourself as the greatest version of yourself, a great leader, leading in alignment with your core values, and leveraging your strengths to lead and inspire others to also be the best versions of themselves and to grow. Imagine yourself on a journey of personal development, constantly checking in and discovering new things about yourself and how your new experiences shape you into who you become. What does this look like? What is your career goal? Is it climbing the corporate ladder to the executive suite or maybe starting your own company? Maybe you've become a great public speaker now, and you provide various training programs for employees to develop their own skills. Or does it look like you becoming a successful mountain climber because you've conquered your fear of heights, and now you help others climb mountains and learn to outgrow their own fears? You probably also train a team to help you, and you now trust them to train others.

Imagine you at your very best, personally and professionally, doing what you love and what makes you happy while using your core values and your strengths and by turning your weaknesses into strengths or improving them to now use them to your advantage. What does this look like to you? Be as descriptive as possible here. Write your heart out on these lines, be bold, be courageous, be brave, be the YOU that you can be and that I know you can be! **Be who you are meant to be as the best version of yourself:**

Now you can lead in alignment with your core values and be the best version of yourself, work towards achieving your goals and your dreams, improve your weaknesses, and be the best that you can be! The possibilities are endless; all you have to do is look inside yourself to understand all that you can do. Never stop practicing self-reflection and understanding how new life experiences change you and shape who you become or how your core values or strengths, or weaknesses shift over time. Never stop personal development and becoming an even better version of yourself; there is no limit to the best that you can be!

Here is a writing exercise that will help you in your leadership and personal development journey throughout your life. It is simple and easy to do at the end of every day. You're going to reflect on 3 things that you did well that day and 3 things that you want to work to improve the next day and include how you are going to improve them the next day. It can be anything from eating healthier or sleeping more to practicing a speech or reading more of a book. This little exercise will help you improve on some aspects of yourself every single day. Think about how much improvement you'd see if you did that every day for one month and actually worked on doing those 3 things better each day. Imagine the improvement after six months or one year! Little improvements each day add up to huge improvements and personal development.

Chapter 6
Overcoming Obstacles

Now when you have your goal or mission in mind and you're on your course of personal development, what happens if you run into challenges or obstacles? How do you get past them and continue on your path? It's going to take inner strength, perseverance, discipline, and passion to make it through challenges, but you can do it.

The first step is to make sure you are very clear on your goal or what you want to accomplish. In the last chapter, you pulled everything together to write your vision of what it looks like when you are the best version of yourself doing what you love and being a great authentic leader. You know how to set goals and work backward by creating every step you would need to take to accomplish that goal. Now I want you to literally visualize that goal and what that looks like, what it feels like, smells like, and sounds like. Turn on epic motivational music on YouTube or Spotify for three minutes. I know that might sound weird, but turn on music that really motivates you. I love epic motivational music from movies or video games. I literally just search "epic motivational music" and put that on for a few minutes. But in your case, find music that deeply motivates or inspires you. Now close your eyes for three minutes and visualize what the best version of you and the great authentic leader feels, sounds, smells, and looks like. Really picture it in your mind until it feels like it's so real you can almost reach your hand out and grab it. Make it tangible; make it feel real.

I want you to do this exercise every morning or whenever you feel in doubt about your dream or goal. And you can and should do this for any and every goal that you set, even small goals. Whenever you need reassurance that you can do it and that you can accomplish your goal, do this exercise. When I do this exercise, I feel so motivated that I'm pretty sure I could climb Mt. Everest the next day or accomplish anything and everything in my wildest dreams. It's so inspiring, and it truly helps my dream or goal become real and tangible.

The next step is to develop your inner strength and determination. There are always going to be challenges or obstacles in your life that you will need to overcome if you want to accomplish your dreams and goals. Sometimes it's bosses or companies. Sometimes it's personal challenges like a toxic relationship that is blocking your path. There will be people who doubt you or question your abilities or even question your dreams. And you absolutely must not listen to them or let them knock you down. There will always be people jealous of what you are going to accomplish because they cannot do it themselves.

So how do you develop your inner strength? Your inner voice is the key here. Your inner voice has to be the coach yelling at you from the sidelines to get back up and keep playing. Your inner voice has to be the one pushing you to keep going and trying harder to do better tomorrow. No one else is going to push you closer to accomplishing your goals and dreams than yourself, even though you may have people who support and cheer you on. You must push yourself harder than anyone else because it's your goal and your dream. If anyone gives you negative criticism or belittles your goals, remind yourself this: would you ask them for life-changing advice and listen only to them? If no, then any opinion less than that should not have an impact on you or slow you down. Constructive feedback is different; I just mean if people try to knock you down, don't let their small opinions get in your way. This is tougher than it sounds, I know. We live in a world where we seek out others' approval with likes and shares, but I need you to get past that to build your inner strength.

If you get stuck, try imagining your inner voice as your favorite coach or motivational speaker who pushes you to persevere and continue working towards your goals. They're with you every step of the way, helping you with every part of your process. Eventually, you won't need to imagine someone else because it'll become part of your inner voice.

The next important step is perseverance and discipline. There will always be challenges and obstacles in life, but you can't let them get you down. Sure, they may slow you down for a bit, and you may need to adjust the steps in your process to account for a new obstacle, but don't quit. There are going to be days when you are tired and exhausted, or you're just not feeling it anymore. On those days, I want you to listen to that motivational music and visualize accomplishing your goal. Discipline is going to get you through those tough days. Discipline is your inner voice telling you to get off the couch and just do it. Discipline is your inner voice telling you to work on that step so that you can move on to the next one and get closer to achieving your goal. It's the coach inside you motivating and inspiring you to push through and get it done. But you must get it done; there are no excuses.

You also want to have very clear steps in your process for accomplishing your goal. Whether it's 5 steps or 20 steps in the process, you need to have very clearly defined steps. That way, if an obstacle does pop up, you know what the next step would be. You can work on finding a different way to achieve that next step, and then the step after that, and so forth.

One of the enemies of discipline is procrastination. You should never put off what you can do now. When I was training for a marathon, I would wake up at 4:30 or 5:00 in the morning every single day. Even on weekdays before work and on cold, rainy days. I had to adjust my schedule to go to sleep earlier, but sometimes when my alarm went off in the morning, I would lay there for a few seconds and question why I was doing this. And then I told myself that I was getting up this early to go running to train for my marathon. I'd visualize crossing the finish line and that feeling of immense accomplishment and happiness and feeling so proud of myself. The moment I'd visualize this, I'd kick my feet out from under my blanket and get ready for my run. Yes, it was brutally early and cold. But I was disciplined in my training, and I made sure my inner voice motivated me, and I practiced my visualization exercise. If I had instead said I'd go running after work, I most likely would not have because I am always exhausted after a long day of work and never want to go run 15 miles after working 9 hours.

A trick to help you stay disciplined is to build something into your daily schedule and make it a habit. I made getting up early to go running a part of my daily schedule, and it became a habit. I dreaded it less and less over time, and it became easier to get up and run or work out. You know your goals, and you know how to create the steps to accomplish that goal and work backward, so how can you make that part of your daily schedule? Whether it's your goal that you wrote about in Chapter

5 or a different goal, think about how you can make the steps in the process part of your daily schedule. Is it writing down in a planner what you did each day to work on that step? Is it getting up early to exercise or read a book or take an online course before you go to work?

Let's practice this with a fairly simple goal and simple steps in the process. Think of something that you want to accomplish, like read and finish a new book, lose 20 pounds, learn a new language, or run a half marathon.

Goal:

Now write the steps you need to accomplish that goal, working backward as we have in the previous chapters. For example, if it's read and finish a new book, maybe you need to:

1. Read every evening before bed for 30 minutes
2. Watch 30 minutes less of the TV, so you have time to read
3. Buy a new book
4. Research a book that might look interesting to read.

So, the steps you need to accomplish your goal are:

____

____

____

____

Now let's take those goals and make them part of your daily routine to turn them into a habit. Are there certain steps that can become part of your daily routine? For instance, in my reading example, you would make the "read every evening before bed for 30 minutes" part of your daily routine. But you would need to actually make that step into a habit, so a great trick is to set an alarm or reminder at 8 pm every day to read for 30 minutes. Alarms are a great way to help a new routine become a habit, but don't just turn off the alarm and keep watching TV! Remember: don't procrastinate. Don't put off for later what you can do now, especially if it's about improving something or working on achieving your goals. So if you need to practice a new language for 15 minutes every evening or read for 30 minutes, maybe you pause your TV show and come back to it later when you get done with your task.

The last thing that you're going to need to help you overcome challenges is passion. You need to be passionate about what you are working on to achieve. When shit gets tough and challenging, and your inner voice is yelling at you to keep pushing, it's going to make it so much easier if you are passionate about what you're achieving. And I'm not talking about completing business management or an HR program that you have to complete for work. I'm talking about your goals and dreams and what you want to achieve; the authentic leadership development or your own personal development goals and dreams you've been working on for this whole book, or any goal that you set for yourself in the future. Make sure that you really want to achieve this goal. Make sure it's something you are passionate about and that you can visualize achieving it. Does it bring you happiness and joy? Accomplishing your goal should make you happy. Even visualizing it in your visualization exercises should make you happy and excited.

I want you to work on building your inner strength, inner voice, discipline, and perseverance through challenges as you work on accomplishing your goals and dreams throughout your entire life. Continue to set goals for yourself, whether they're massive goals or smaller goals, whether they take a year to achieve, or simply a month. Use your inner strength, voice, and discipline to work through each step in your process. And when you've achieved that goal, I want you to set another goal. Set an even bigger or more challenging goal, so you continue to grow your skills and improve aspects of yourself. Never stop pushing yourself to be the best version of yourself because there is no limit, and you can continue to grow and grow and become better and better. There is nothing you can't do if you put your mind, passion, and perseverance into accomplishing a goal.

Endnotes

Chapter 1

1. Huckabee Sarkaria, P. (2018). Authentic leadership. In
    McManus, R.M., Ward, S.J., & Perry, A.K.
    (Eds.). *Ethical leadership: A primer*. Cheltenham, UK:
    Edward Elgar. Chapter 12 (pp. 241-265).

Chapter 2

2. Porter, J. (2019, June 19). *How to move from self-
    awareness to self-improvement*. Harvard Business
    Review. Retrieved January 20, 2022, from
    https://hbr.org/2019/06/how-to-move-from-self-
    awareness-to-self-improvement

Chapter 4

3. Institute for Health and Human Potential. (n.d.). *The
    Meaning of Emotional Intelligence*. IHHP. Retrieved
    January 20, 2022, from
    https://www.ihhp.com/meaning-of-emotional-
    intelligence/

About the Author

Alexa Starks holds a Master of Arts degree in Organizational Leadership with a Concentration in Ethics from Claremont Lincoln University and a High-Performance Leadership Certificate from Cornell University. She has a passion for helping others become the best version of themselves and recognize their full potential in life. Alexa lives in Dallas, Texas, with her husband, Wayne.

Connect

@alexastarkscoaching

www.alexastarks.com